A walk from
Our City School

Deborah Chancellor • Chris Fairclough

W
FRANKLIN WATTS
LONDON • SYDNEY

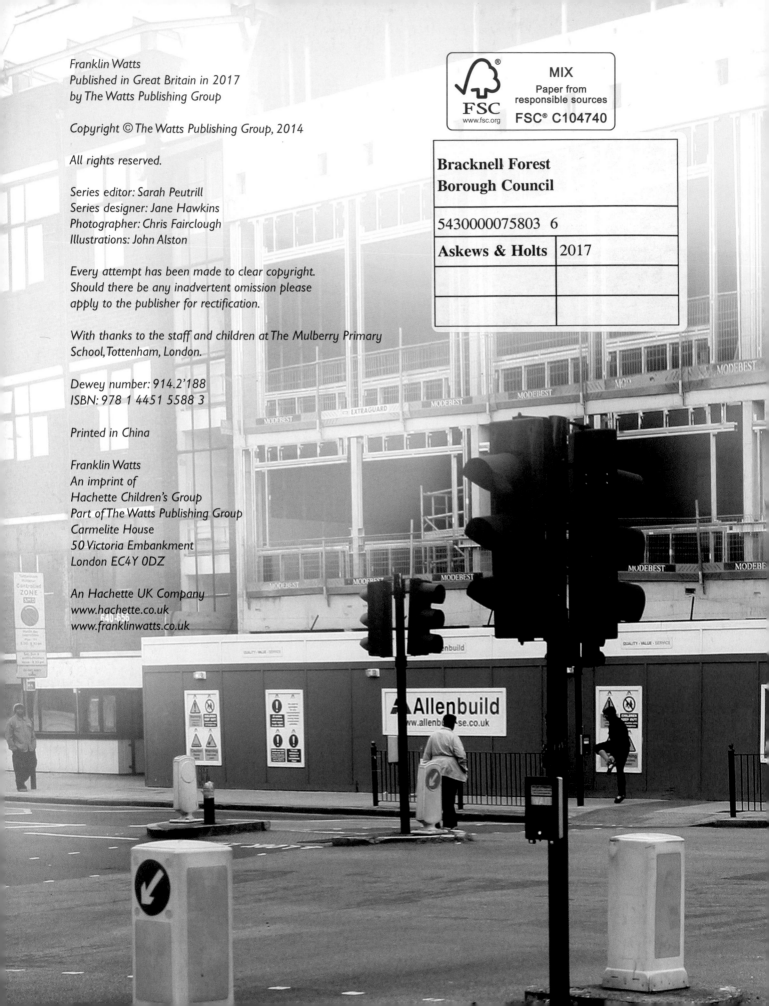

Contents

City walk	6
Starting out	8
Busy road	10
Train station	12
City life	14
At the park	16
Finding the way	18
The High Road	20
Local work	22
Back to school	24
Around the world	26
Find the route	28
Glossary	29
Index	30

Words in **bold** are in the glossary on page 29.

City walk

Ranaa, Oliwia, Daniel and Owais want to explore their **local** area. They decide to go on a walk from their school. The children live in London, the **capital city** of the **UK**. Their school is called The Mulberry Primary School and it is in an area called Tottenham, to the north of the city.

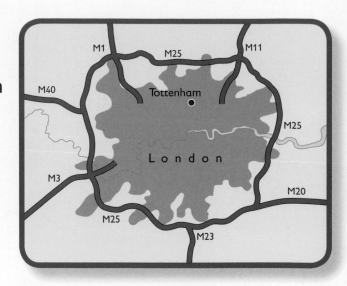

FOCUS ON GEOGRAPHY
London is the largest city in Europe with the biggest **population**. This huge city is home to over eight million people.

Before they set off, the children plan their walk carefully. To work out their **route**, they look at maps on the Internet and local street maps.

It is important to plan a safe and interesting walk.

FOCUS ON SPORT

Tottenham is home to a Premier League football club called Tottenham Hotspur (Spurs). The club's **stadium** is near to the school. People come from all over the country to watch football matches there.

White Hart Lane stadium is where Spurs play football.

The children have some questions about Tottenham that they would like to answer. They write these questions down, so they remember what to look out for.

Q1 Is there much traffic on the roads?

Q2 What kinds of public transport are there?

Q3 What kinds of home do people live in?

Q4 What sorts of shop are there?

Q5 What jobs do people do?

Tottenham High Road is always busy with traffic.

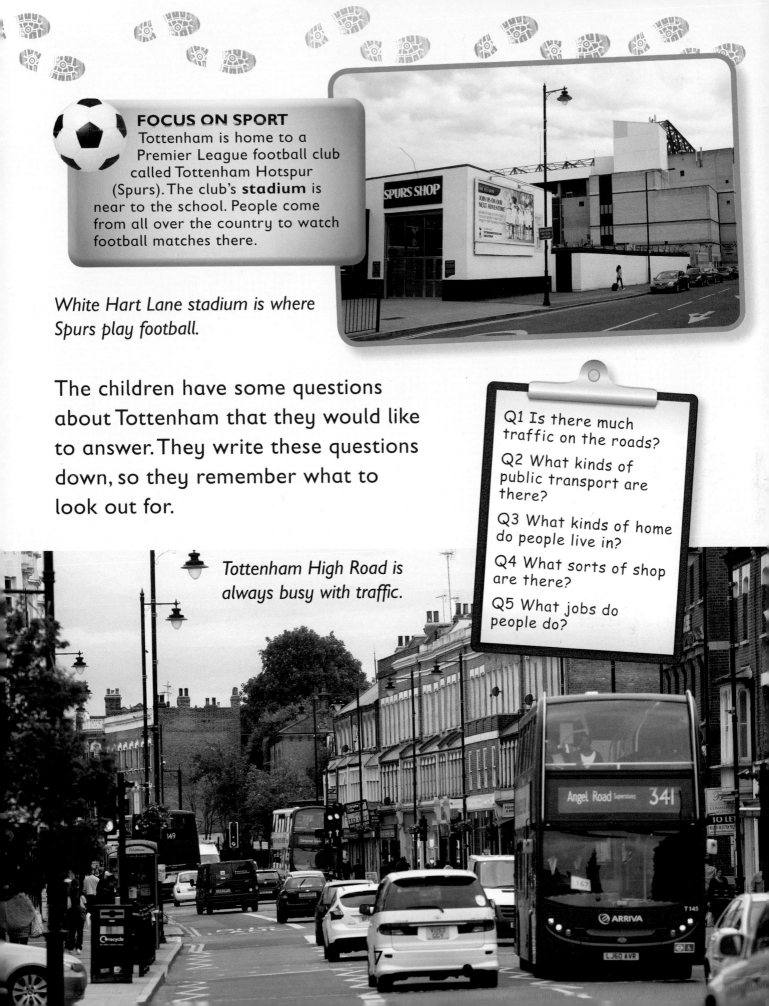

Starting out

Before the children and their teacher set off, Ranaa and Daniel set up **pedometers**. This is to measure how far they walk. They also pack a street map, a camera and a **smartphone** with **GPS**, to help them track their route.

The group leaves through the main school entrance and turns into Parkhurst Road.

Parkhurst Road is lined with houses.

PARKHURST ROAD N.17

Many cars are parked on Parkhurst Road.

Parkhurst Road is a long, straight road. After walking for a few minutes, the children come to a crossroads. They cross the road and turn right, walking along Dowsett Road towards the High Road.

? Is your school on a busy street like this one?

Busy road

The children come to some traffic lights and turn left onto the High Road. This main road is also called the A1010.

*The children look at the street map and see that the High Road heads south towards **central** London.*

The group walk past some shops. There is a lot of traffic, but it is not as heavy as it is in the **rush hour**. This is when people travel to and from work in the morning and evening.

Q1: Is there much traffic on the roads?

A: The roads are busy with cars, vans, bikes and buses.

The children stop to look at the traffic. They count all the different kinds of **vehicles** on the road. They see cars, vans, bikes, motorbikes and buses.

London is famous for its red double-decker buses.

Focus on History

A hundred and fifty years ago, there were carts, carriages and **omnibuses** on the roads of London. Most vehicles were pulled along by horses. There were no cars, motorbikes or double-decker buses.

Train station

Ranaa, Oliwia, Daniel and Owais cross the road to reach a train station called Bruce Grove.

There is a **Victorian** post box in the wall. This tells them the station was built in the time of Queen Victoria.

'VR' on the post box stands for Victoria Regina, or Queen Victoria.

The station is next to some traffic lights.

Trains from Bruce Grove station take passengers south to central London, or north to the **suburbs**. It is midday, so there are not many people at the station. Fewer people are going to work now.

? Is there a train station near where you live?

There is a railway bridge next to the station. The children use the GPS on their teacher's smartphone to track their position and see the railway bridge on the map. They walk under the bridge, along a road called the A10. This road leads north out of London.

Daniel and Ranaa spot a street sign. It tells them this section of the A10 is called Bruce Grove, like the train station.

BRUCE GROVE N.17

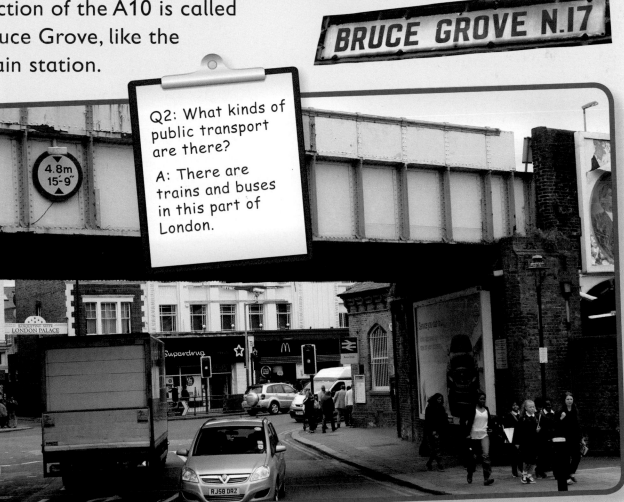

4.8m
15′-9″

Q2: What kinds of public transport are there?

A: There are trains and buses in this part of London.

City life

On Bruce Grove the children walk past some shops that sell food from different countries.

People who live in this part of London come from all over the world and enjoy eating a variety of food.

The group walk north for about ten minutes. They pass some **residential** roads, with houses and tall blocks of flats. Some homes look modern and others look old.

Q3: What kind of home do people live in?

A: People live in houses and flats. Some are new and some are old.

14

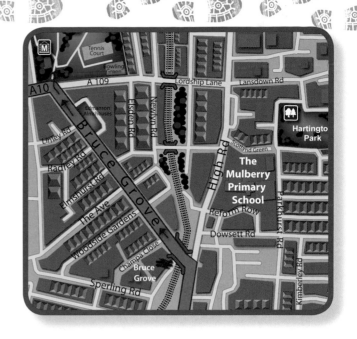

These *almshouses* provide homes for old people.

The children come to a **junction**. On the other side of the road they see a park called Bruce Castle Park. They cross at a zebra crossing and go into the park.

FOCUS ON SCIENCE
Cities need green spaces, where people can go to relax and take exercise. Trees and plants also help to clean up **polluted** city air.

At the park

Ranaa, Oliwia, Daniel and Owais like coming to Bruce Castle Park. It is good to get away from the busy roads. There are lots of trees in the park, and the children spot some squirrels and birds in the branches.

Some people are walking and jogging in the park. There are places for playing sport, such as football, tennis and basketball.

The play area in the park has some great climbing equipment.

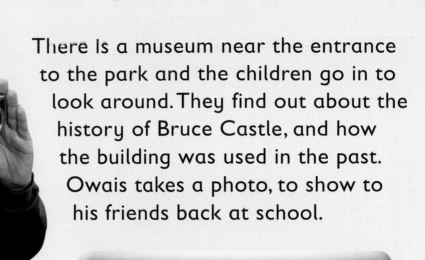

There Is a museum near the entrance to the park and the children go in to look around. They find out about the history of Bruce Castle, and how the building was used in the past. Owais takes a photo, to show to his friends back at school.

? Is there a park or a **sports ground** near you?

Focus on History

Parts of Bruce Castle are about 500 years old, dating back to when Henry VIII was king of England. In Victorian times, Bruce Castle was used as a school and today it is a museum.

Finding the way

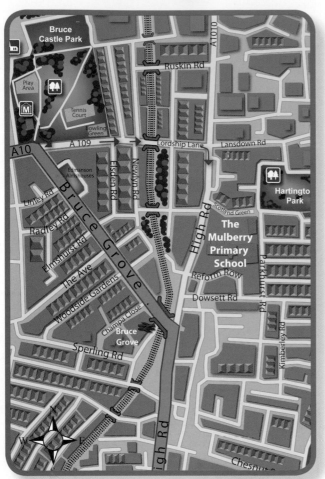

The children check their position on the map. They need to go east to get back to the High Road, so Owais looks at a **compass**. The needle of the compass points north, so from this he works out which way is east.

Street maps are very useful in towns and cities.

LORDSHIP LANE N.17.

The group turn left down a road called Lordship Lane. They pass a few bus stops along the way and walk under another railway bridge. On the map, they notice that this is the same **railway line** that runs through Bruce Grove station.

Soon the children reach a crossroads. They are back at the High Road. They cross carefully at the traffic lights and turn right, walking south down the High Road.

? Are there any traffic lights near your school?

The High Road

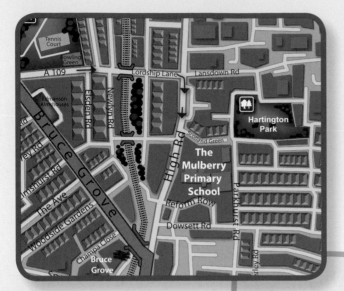

The group pass a building site on the corner of the High Road where some new flats are being built. A big **crane** is lifting heavy materials. Then the children walk past some offices. There are lots of different kinds of buildings.

Focus on History

The High Road in Tottenham is a very old road, but it has not always had this name. Parts of it are on the route of Ermine Street, a **Roman** road that went from London to Lincoln and York.

Many bus routes stop along Tottenham High Road.

20

After a few minutes the children come to some shops. They count how many of each kind of shop they see, for example the number of food shops and **newsagents**. They want to know which sort of shop is the most common. Back at school, they will use this information to draw a bar chart.

The High Road is always busy with shoppers.

Q4: What sorts of shops are there?

A: There are many different shops, such as mini markets and clothes shops.

Fruit and vegetables are on display outside this mini market.

Local work

There are many **businesses** on the High Road, such as cafés, restaurants and hairdressers. Businesses give work to local people. They also provide people with a useful service, for example you can go to a **travel agent** to book a holiday.

Ranaa, Oliwia, Daniel and Owais think about all the jobs people do in the city. Their teacher reminds them that some people work in hospitals, schools and offices.

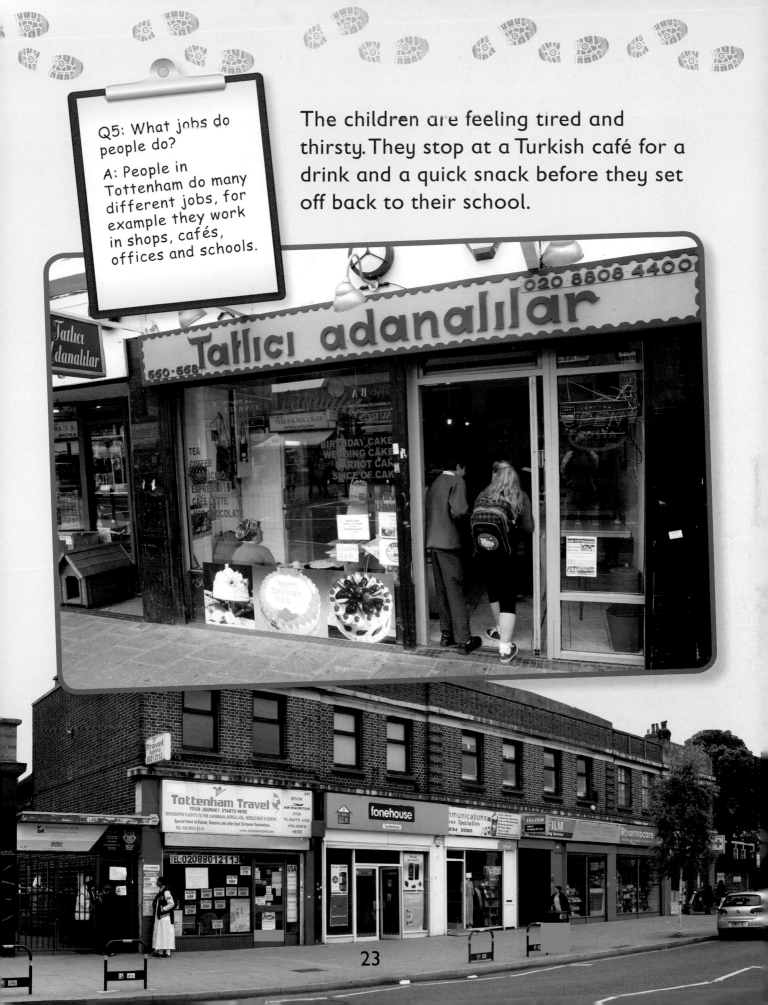

Q5: What jobs do people do?

A: People in Tottenham do many different jobs, for example they work in shops, cafés, offices and schools.

The children are feeling tired and thirsty. They stop at a Turkish café for a drink and a quick snack before they set off back to their school.

Buck to school

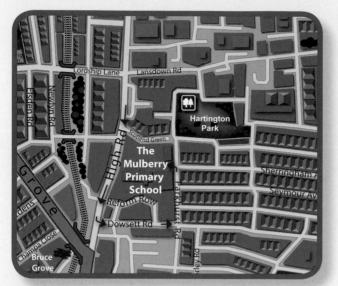

Oliwia checks the group's position on their teacher's smartphone. She can see that they have not got much further to go now. They continue walking down the High Road until they reach the turning with Dowsett Road.

FOCUS ON TECHNOLOGY

Smartphones can help you find your way around and show you where you are. You can download apps to help you **navigate**, and see how far you have walked.

The group take a left turn, walking east along Dowsett Road. When they reach the zebra crossing, they walk north up Parkhurst Road. There are signs on this road to slow down traffic and make the road safer.

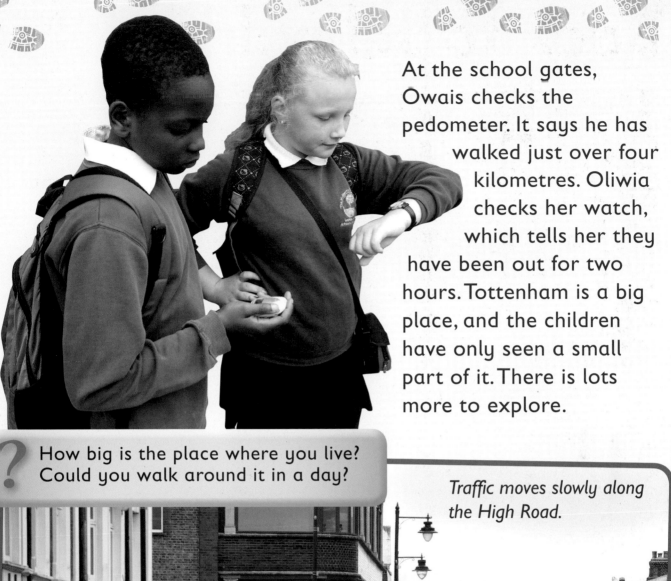

At the school gates, Owais checks the pedometer. It says he has walked just over four kilometres. Oliwia checks her watch, which tells her they have been out for two hours. Tottenham is a big place, and the children have only seen a small part of it. There is lots more to explore.

? How big is the place where you live? Could you walk around it in a day?

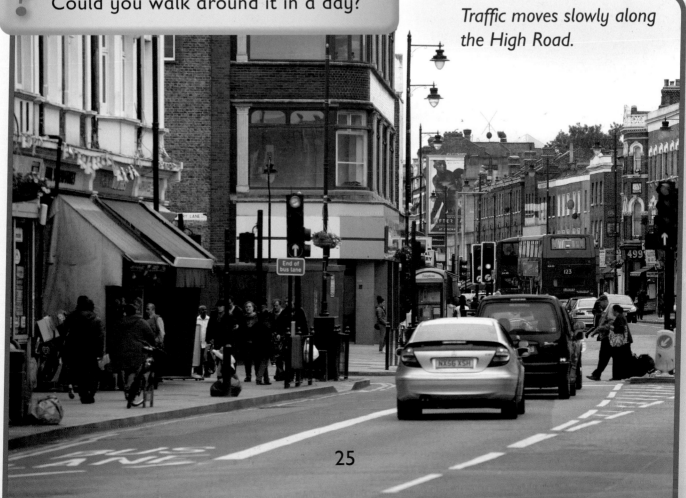

Traffic moves slowly along the High Road.

Around the world

The people who live in London come from all around the world. About 100,000 people live in Tottenham. They speak many different **languages**. At The Mulberry Primary School, 49 languages are spoken. When the children play and work together, they usually speak in English.

FOCUS ON GEOGRAPHY
Tottenham is a very **multi-cultural** place. Over 175 languages are spoken in this part of London.

? Do any of your friends speak a different language to you?

Mulberry Primary School is linked with Chimweta Primary School in a country called Malawi, in southeast Africa. Oliwia, Daniel and Owais look for the **continent** of Africa on a world map.

Mr Kelly enjoyed meeting the children at Chimweta School.

The children like to find out about life in Malawi. One of their teachers, Mr Kelly, has been to visit Chimweta Primary School, and has met the teachers and children there. This school is in a big town called Salima, in central Malawi.

Find the route

Can you follow the whole route on the map?

Where are each of the places shown in the photos?

1 LORDSHIP LANE N.17.

2

3

4

5

6

7

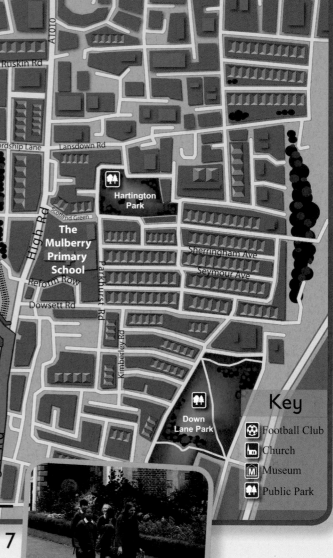

Tottenham Hotspur FC

Bruce Castle Park

Play Area

Tennis Court

Bowling Green

Ruskin Rd

Lordship Lane

Lansdown Rd

A10

A 109

Elmanson Almshouses

Linley Rd

Bruce Grove

Radley Rd

Elmhurst Rd

The Ave

Woodside Gardens

Champa Close

Bruce Grove

Sperling Rd

Elsden Rd

Newlyn Rd

High Rd

Scotland Green

The Mulberry Primary School

Hartington Park

Reform Row

Dowsett Rd

Parkhurst Rd

Kimberley Rd

Sherringham Ave

Seymour Ave

Down Lane Park

High Rd

100m

Key
⚽ Football Club
⛪ Church
Ⓜ Museum
🌳 Public Park

Glossary

almshouses housing for the elderly, or for other people in need

business a firm that makes things or provides a service, eg a café

capital city main city in a country

central middle of something

compass instrument that shows where north is

continent one of the world's main land masses

crane machine that moves and lifts heavy objects

GPS network of satellites that tell you where you are on Earth

junction place where roads join together

language the words or phrases used by a group of people to communicate with each other, such as French, English, Spanish etc

local nearby, in the neighbourhood

multi-cultural with many different cultures, traditions and religions

newsagent shop that sells newspapers and magazines

omnibus old fashioned word for bus

pedometer a machine that measures how far you walk or run

polluted made dirty and unhealthy

population number of people who live in a place

railway line track that a train runs along

residential where people live

Roman from the time of the ancient Romans (43–410)

route the way you go to reach a place

rush hour time when traffic is at its busiest

smartphone mobile phone with computer power and the Internet

sports ground place where people play sport

stadium sports ground surrounded by seats for fans

suburbs places to live on the edge of a city or town

travel agent place where you can book a holiday or journey

vehicle a means of transport, such as a bus, bike or car

Victorian dating back to the time of Queen Victoria (1837–1901)

UK The United Kingdom – together the countries England, Scotland, Wales and Northern Ireland

Index

Bruce Castle Museum 17
Bruce Castle Park 15–17
Bruce Grove 12–15
building site 20
buses 11, 13, 19, 20
businesses 22–23

Ermine Street 20

football 7, 16

GPS 8, 13

Henry VIII 17
High Road 7, 9, 10, 18, 19, 20,
  21, 22, 24, 25
homes 7, 8, 14–15

jobs 7, 22, 23

languages 26, 27
London 6, 10, 11, 12, 13, 14,
  20, 26

Malawi 27
museum 17

offices 20, 22, 23

park 15–17
population (of London) 6
public transport 7, 12–13

Queen Victoria 12

railway bridge 13, 19
railway line 19

schools 6, 7, 8, 9, 17, 19, 21, 22,
  23, 24, 25, 26, 27
shops 7, 11, 14, 21, 23
sport 7, 16, 17

Tottenham Hotspur (Spurs) 7
train station 12–13, 19
trains 12, 13
traffic 7, 11, 24, 25

world maps 26–27